THE HIMALAYAN
My journey from Bhutan to America

Nar Pradhan

Published by:

Alch Management LLC
Cleveland, OH 44111
Email: info@alchmanagement.com

Editor: Eric Impion

Email: eimpion@gmail.com

First Edition: February 20218

ISBN-13: 9782900085271

Printed in the United States of America

I dedicate this book to those who lose hope for the future and are about to give up. To them, I want to remind what President Franklin D. Roosevelt said, "We have always held to the hope, the belief, the conviction that there is a better life, a better world, beyond the horizon."

CONTENTS

FOREWORD

I first met the Bhutanese refugee community in August 2009 when I was asked if I would like to volunteer as an ESOL teacher through Building Hope in the City, a non-profit in Cleveland, Ohio. At that time, I was working as an Enterprise Architect for a Fortune 500 company and thought, sure, that sounds like it could be fun! Little did I know that one decision has the power to change your life.

Like many people born in America, I had little to no understanding of the refugee experience. I had heard the word in passing but never given it any thought until I met the people behind the word. My heart was broken as I began to realize what it meant to be without a home and a country. To be forced to flee everything that was familiar, to leave behind everything that reminded you of home and family, to run into the unknown with nothing but the clothes on your back and your children. I asked myself, how is it possible that I had lived my life with little to no understanding of the world? The answer came quickly, the sad truth is that it's because you are American and these problems aren't on the shores of your country, or in the villages of your land.

As I began to get to know them, the Bhutanese people began to hold a special place in my heart. The smiles of the older men and women, quick to offer candy and a traditional greeting, Namaste Teacher. The laughter, the music, the dancing, the food quickly became as much a part of me as the students. I had found a new home and a new people.

I met Nar almost a year after he came to America and we have been friends ever since. His gentle spirit and love for his community are evident from the first moment you meet him. I have turned to the Pradhan family many times for help and support as we work together to build a strong refugee community in our area. They were instrumental in helping us to launch The Hope Center for Refugees and Immigrants, a community center and school based in Cleveland that seeks to help people move from surviving to thriving.

Many times, the word refugee is used as a synonym for poor, worthless, uneducated but those are only labels given by people who haven't met them. Strong, resilient, courageous, these are the words that best describe the people who have survived the worst of what the world can throw at them and still find it within them to start over in America, bringing with them the beauty of their culture and transplanting it into our neighborhoods with restaurants, grocery stores, and boutiques.

Many people who come are hesitant to remember the past; the joyful memories of family are often mixed with the painful memories of separation. Nar's journey is a window into the story of the refugee; a story of simplicity, followed by heartache and ultimately triumph over his circumstances. This is the true story of the refugee, the people I am honored to call not only my friends but my family.

Eileen Wilson, Director of

The Hope Center for Refugees and Immigrants
Cleveland, Ohio

ACKNOWLEDGEMENT

The writing of this book involved the assistance of many friends and family members to whom I am really grateful. I would like to thank them for constantly encouraging me during the course of this project, which I couldn't have completed without their support and continuous encouragement.

First of all, I would like to thank my lovely wife Saru who strongly encouraged me to write this book and whose continuous help throughout this journey has been invaluable. My profound gratitude goes to my beloved sister Mrs. Damanta Pradhan and my brother in law Mr. Bhupathi Pradhan, who did extraordinary work in bringing to life my story, I can't imagine how I could ever repay them. They tirelessly edited, suggested, and supported me to be here, very proud to have finished this book.

In addition, my friend Eileen Wilson has provided significant support by adding the final touches to the story before the publishing, I am really appreciative of her in my life. I am really grateful for the opportunity to participate in this project as it has helped me to improve my skills. I am glad that I was able to provide valuable insight on this project.

I would like to express my special thanks to my editor Eric Impion who inspired me and gave me the golden opportunity to do this wonderful project which also helped me do a lot of research and allowed me to recall fond memories from my childhood and current life in this book.

Lastly, I will forever be grateful to my lovely Mom (Padma) and Dad (Lt. Ishor) who brought me into this beautiful world! Without you, I would never have been the person I am today. My love for you is immeasurable. I am thankful for the guidance and love you have given and continued to give me. Thank you for everything!

1
CHILDHOOD WITH YOUR FATHER

My story began in Bhutan which is a small landlocked mountainous country between Tibet (China) and India. It has some of the most fertile lands on earth and the majority of the population are farmers. People can be poor but happy and filled with profound joy in their day-to-day life. It was a country without beggars or homeless people. All the people were hard-working and didn't have to worry about their basic needs, though we lacked modern technology.

Our tiny village of Toribari was at the peak of development as a health clinic (dispensary), an office of agriculture, telephone service, a supply of electricity, a water facility, a primary level school, and a few transportation facilities had made their way there.

One of our villager's son who belongs to the Ghalley family studied in Canada. He was the only one who had a television in his house. We used to watch movies once a week which was the only option to learn about the outside world. We all were happy and excited about the opportunity to watch television at his house and get more information about the world.

One night, as usual, we were watching television. It was such a scary moment, everybody was enjoying watching the movie; you couldn't hear a pin drop and suddenly, the police came and tried to seize the TV! However, the owner (an educated man) fortunately managed to handle the situation. In Bhutan, a country with a One Nation, One Peoples' policy, the general public was prohibited from watching and even owning a television. Even with situations such as this, my life as a child was idyllic.

I was born the sixth child of my mother Padma and my father Lt. Iswor Pradhan and was pronounced, soon after birth, a healthy baby. In those days, there was a problem with giving birth due to a lack of maternal knowledge and heavy workloads for the mothers. My mother was blessed with eight healthy children, my older sisters Kumari, Hari, Bishnu, and Damanti, my older brother Dhan and my younger siblings, Narayan and Nithya (Dil).

My father was a visionary businessman and an active farmer and would stay busy almost all the time for the betterment of the family, the people in need, and the larger community. My Mother used to conceptualize continuing business carried out by the father. In order to help and provide villagers with good service, my parents started a grocery business where many types of food products and grocery items were made available locally instead of having to walk a far distance to the market in the big cities.

Life was so splendid and joyful. We had everything we needed and could help people in need, the environment was so peaceful and calm.

One Sunday evening, I was playing with my friend when his mother told him, "Stop playing and come home, you have to be ready for school, early tomorrow morning." We stopped playing and went to our respective homes. I didn't know what school was about but, in my mind, I had to wake up early in the morning and follow them. I didn't sleep well that night. When I woke up, my mother was serving breakfast to my elder brothers and sisters for school. I was sitting at the ladder curiously watching my friend's house when they came out for school. No one bothered me sitting on the ladder.

At that time, my friend and his mother came out of his house, and immediately, I went out of my house softly tiptoeing. I walked slowly and followed them for a little distance, and finally, I ran towards them and called my friend (Jiwan). His mom was shocked and told me to go back home, but it was almost a mile away and I insisted on going with them. While in the middle of the path my elder brother was surprised to see me with them. My friend's mother explained the situation and after knowing the story behind it I followed them and he did not yell at me, instead he helped me to cross the two small rivers.

At the school, all the students were standing in a line and then they went to their respective classrooms. We sat on the ground and my friend's mom went to the office to enroll him. I was wondering if I could also join my friend in his class at school but the criteria for school age was six years old, and I was a few months shy of six at that time. When I got home, I kept insisting that my father enroll me in school. The next day, my father took me to school, carrying me on his shoulders, and registered my name too, which was a vivid memory in my life.

In those days, in order to enter school, some questions were asked by the teacher and I needed to answer them correctly. Questions such as, how many legs does a cow have? How many eyes does a cow have? How many tails does a cow have? and so on. In my first attempt, I was unable to answer all the questions that were asked of me. However, in my second attempt, I practiced and answered correctly. As the saying goes, "practice makes perfect". Happily, I did and succeeded the second time.

I was enrolled in LKG (Lower Kindergarten) because there was no preschool system in those days. Every morning, my father held my hand; sometimes carrying me on his back, walking me to school, and bringing me home along with my other siblings. It was five kilometers away from my house one way with limited public transportation facilities at that time.

On the way to school, Dad used to tell me stories to encourage me not to do negative things and also not to harm my friends. While coming home, he would ask me what I had learned. To minimize his tiredness, he would often chant a beautiful Nepali folk song in his charming voice. He would say, "One day, I will buy a red car for all of us." We had a good time playing with him. My dad loved children so much we couldn't even fathom. He would say," My children are my gods and goddesses."

I felt I was in heaven, having the guidance of perfect parents set in the most peaceful surrounding of the most beautiful country in the world as if it was a seed in the fertile land. My parents always encouraged me to do good work and inspired all of us to think about all matters positively. Good work and a positive attitude would pay the dividend of a worthy and quality life in the days to come.

My parents were always busy focusing on their daily duties and the responsibilities of the business and the farms, as well as helping travelers who were sick and seeking basic needs or some financial help to reach their destination. "Pradhan Shop" was the only shop in the entire village. Included in it were a grocery, restaurant, and bar.

According to my mother and other villagers, some ill willed people burnt down our shop three different times. The third time, my parents woke up and found the whole house on fire. To save their children, they broke windows and doors and we narrowly escaped from the fire. Both of my parents sacrificed a lot for the betterment of their children. I heartily thank my parents for their hard work that they did in those days. Although my father is not on this earth, I believe my dad's soul is still around in the universe.

Once again, I want to salute him and my mom because of their blessing and encouragement.

Because of them, I stand here today on my own two feet. Those days spent as a child playing in the middle of the road with my friends and siblings in our beautiful village will never be wiped out of my memory and will always remain fresh in my mind.

2
LIFE WITHOUT OUR FATHER

It was winter, the weather was chilly outside. I heard the unusual sounds of our dog named Bhattu barking and the odd noise of a bird chirping. I knew from my mom, that my dad was severely sick with pneumonia. He was admitted to the Geylegphug General Hospital and then after about a week he was discharged and sent back home. Soon after he arrived, my mom did cultural rituals to save my father's life but to no avail.

A couple of days later, my mother grabbed me and my younger brother from our bed and took us to see our father. He was sleeping on the floor and there was a coin on his forehead. We saw some relatives crying but we did not have any idea what was going on. My youngest brother and I started playing in the room. I noticed that people were gathering outside but children were not allowed to go outside and see the activities. We were innocent but felt happy that more and more people were staying in our house day and night; blissfully unaware of why our elder brother, mother, and other relatives were wearing a loose long unstitched white cloth which we wear while mourning a death in a family. All my family members, except my eldest sister, neighbors, and relatives were gathered to mourn my father.

One evening, my eldest sister was dropped by the bus from Yamphula in northern Bhutan. Soon after she heard the news of my dad's passing, she started crying. I was so curious to ask why she was crying. I didn't have any concept about death. One of our neighbors came and explained the situation. I was totally stunned. Days passed and we did not see our father and I finally realized that he was not physically with us. I was thinking that I would do anything to get my father back, but that was a different reality. Losing my father at the tender age of six left a huge void in my life though my mother played a dual role to provide both a mother and a father's love.

Sometimes, life seems very unfair, each step is uncertain so love and respect your near and dear ones, help each other as much as you can. The best part of Nepali culture is that when someone dies, all the villagers help the family financially and physically until the ritual ceremony is done. This is the heart of my culture.

After my father's death, my mother had to bear all the responsibility of taking care of the business and farms, along with the needs of her many young children when she was only 38 years old. My elder brother Dhan who was a substitute father, was only eleven years old, while my eldest sister, Kumari, had already gotten married and left the home. Carrying that weight of responsibility was very tough for my mom and she closed some of the businesses, including the grocery. Day by day, my mother was unable to take care of the cardamom gardens located in three different areas though she was still taking care of the rice and cornfields, two orange gardens, and one cardamom garden. Our splendid life became very difficult, but my mom did not lose her hope; she loved us and filled the gap left by the loss of our father.

Life went on, my elder brothers at their young age took the initiative to raise their younger siblings. We continued at school and one day, when I was in the first grade, a student who sat near me brought an egg to give to the teacher. When I took my book from my bag, my hand touched his bag and the egg fell to the floor and broke. After that, he and his friends started bullying me and told me to bring one rupee to school otherwise I would be punished. When I forgot to bring money the next day, they beat me and said that I had to bring two rupees.

At that time, our shop was still running and after I reached home, I had to get the money. I went into the shop and asked my mom to give me one rupee and went to school the next day and gave it to them, but they still threatened and punished me. Bullying by the stronger group to the weaker group prevailed. Those days were a nightmare.

My third eldest sister, Bishnu, noticed the change in me and asked what was going on. I told her everything and she slapped one of the bullies on the face and told the group that if they did it again, they would not escape her wrath. My sister was very energetic and if it happened that she needed to fight with boys, she was ever ready. After that, they left me alone.

In the second grade, one of the chapters that I studied in my Nepali textbook was entitled "Columbus discovered America". After we got back from school, we were playing with friends in front of our house and I still remember thinking, how is that America? When viewing the sun as it was about to set on the horizon, I was visualizing America; I had a vivid picture in my mind. Someday, I will be going to America. That was my innocent thought after reading that lesson.

To help my mother, every morning my fourth eldest sister, Damanti, and I woke up early in the morning, around 4 am, and tried to prepare breakfast. Sometimes, we cooked it well and sometimes not very well due to our lack of knowledge about cooking, but we tried our best to make breakfast for our other siblings and we all ate together as a family. Walking every morning to school and back home was nearly five kilometers; it was good exercise but tiring. Sometimes, I would run to compete with my friends. While we were walking, when we saw a car, truck, or jeep pass by we would stop and chant a slogan by joining hands "Leopani Daju, Leopani Daju" while going to school in the morning. And while going back home we would also chant a song "Toribari Daju, Toribari Daju". Those songs we chanted were to try and get a ride from the passing transportation.

The weather was always a challenge as we walked to school. In the summer, it consisted of heavy rainfall causing two of the rivers, the Dholkhola and Leokhola, to rise. We had to cross them to reach the school and to avoid getting drenched from heavy rainfall and running the risk of crossing the swollen river, students from our village would rent a house near to the school.

I still remember the day, one early morning around 3 a.m., a man from a political group came and knocked on our door and notified my mom that she needed to go to a rally in Sarbhang District. I was only in the third grade, he showed up with a sharp knife and told us tomorrow at 7 a.m., everyone above 10 years old and below 60 years had to go to a rally. A second group would come during the rally to check the houses and if they found anyone at home of that age, other than sick people, we would lose six inches (indicating that they would chop off our heads). That day, we were about to go to school when a group of people told us that our school will be closing and if they found us outside, we would be killed; after hearing this from the activist groups, we stopped going to school and came back home.

After that, I saw a group of people marching on the road peacefully protesting with a slogan promoting democracy. People participated from remote villages and urban settings too. The next day, a truck full of people came from another city with a burning signboard and burned the Bhutanese National dress, "Kira and

Gho". They behaved aggressively and some of
the old people and young people from our
village were forcefully put into a truck and
taken to Sarbhang district office. While my
school was still open, I remember seeing Nepali
textbooks being burned in my school. I did not
understand the heads and tails of that incident
but in my mind, I was thinking something was
wrong.

Schools remained closed and we were deprived
of formal education at a young age. We did not
have any option to do anything after that, so we
started helping our parents and became
cowboys. Being a cowboy at nine years old
made life interesting and enjoyable. We took
the cows to the jungle and swam during the
daytime in the river. In the evening, we
collected the cows and brought them to the
house. Sometimes, with our neighbor and my
brothers, we made a trap for wild chickens in
the forest. We used to collect wild fruits,
vegetables, and wild chickens that we trapped
in the forest and brought them home to make
curry for my family.

My younger brother and I went to see the trap and in it, was a baby tiger that jumped toward us to attack! The trap consisted of a piece of string attached to a plant that was bent and would snap back when the string was pulled free by an animal. Luckily, the tiger was already in one of our traps and had broken the plant, and his right leg was caught in the plant and tied with the trap rope. We were so afraid that we cut the plants and made strong rods and started hitting them. We knew that it was either him or us; either he would kill us, or we had to kill him. He was so aggressive and attempted to kill us several times but finally, after almost an hour, we killed him by breaking 10 to 15 strong rods made by the plant. We tied his leg with the rope and one of us pulled him along and one of us walked behind, still thinking that it was a baby tiger.

On the way home, we met one of the villagers and told him proudly that we killed a baby tiger. He looked and said that it was a male wild cat, which is a very dangerous animal but fortunately, your brothers are still alive. He said that he wanted to take it because he wanted his male parts for some special purpose, and we gave it to him. Day by day, we became experts at playing in the jungle. When we had our Khukuris, a traditional Nepali knife, with us we were never afraid of anything in the dense jungle.

Sometimes, I went with my mom when she climbed big trees to cut branches to feed the cows and goats; we were experts in climbing trees. My father had built a border around our land with a stone wall and there was a huge tree with two big branches that overlooked the wall. My younger brothers and I climbed the tree and decided to go to each of the branches and sing 'Jhapa Jane Gadi', a famous slogan for little kids like us to chant as we saw people start to leave Bhutan and head for Jhapa, Nepal in trucks provided by India, to become refugees due to the increasing political issues.

I had a bad fall during which I injured my back. Though my back was hurting, we decided not to tell anyone; if anyone knew about the accident, we would have been punished. From that day on, I learned a lesson and stopped climbing the tree. Soon after that, my mom became ill and, in the morning, my elder sibling took her to the hospital at Geylegphug which was 15 kilometers away from our village and she was hospitalized.

The next day the doctor brought in the test results and said that my mom had been diagnosed with chronic bronchitis (asthma). I stayed with my mom to take care of her. The hospital staff was very helpful, time and again they came and examined my mom and reminded me to give her the medication. I have fond memories of swapping stories with the other caregivers. While we were sharing our individual stories and our positive experiences, sick patients were happy and had a positive attitude. They expressed that they felt relief from some of the pain. The hospital provided breakfast, lunch, and dinner for the sick people, but my mother loved homemade food rather than hospital food. For the sake of my mom, I used to cook and bring her homemade food.

After six weeks in the hospital, my mother was discharged. She came home, along with the prescriptions, paperwork, and follow up summary. That experience impressed on me the important role hope has in lifting the spirits of those who were sick.

3

THE CHILDREN'S WORK

In our backyard, we had many varieties of fruits and green leafy vegetables growing in the garden. Among the other fruits such as mango, oranges, and coconuts, one of the most popular fruits was lychee. When I was eight years old, my younger brother Narayan and I used to pick lychee fruit and sell it to travelers at the bus stop. One day, while we were selling lychee, a white foreigner got off the bus and took a picture of us. We both were so excited and happy when we had our photo taken.

Even as a child, I knew that we had two great festivals we celebrated grandly each year (Dasara & Diwali). Festival time was a time to make all our family members happy and gather with relatives both far and near. During our festival, we used to get new clothes, eat delicious food, and have fun watching folk dance and singing programs. We shared with each other the successes and challenges that we faced in our day to day life.

After our festival, everybody resumed their regular tasks. During the winter, my older brother Dhan and Birendra, my cousin's brother, left home to do seasonal work such as carrying oranges from the garden to the place where they would be stored. From the money they earned, my brothers would buy clothes and basic necessities for our family. Our village was between two big cities, 16 kilometers to Sarbhang and 15 kilometers to Geylegphug. People from the mountains and from the rural areas used to come to the cities for shopping. They would walk one, two, and sometimes three days to get there while others who were well off would ride their horses.

In rural areas there was no means of transportation, the rich people used horses to carry their items while poor people had to carry the load by themselves. People mostly bought rice, spices, oil, and salt. One of our friends and his brother had a business selling bread and tea. This inspired my brother Narayan and me to also start a business. In order to start up our small enterprise, my elder sister, Kumari, gave us money to invest in our small bakery business. The bakery products we sold were produced in India, so we picked them up from the border between Geylegphug, Bhutan, and Dath Ghari, India.

After packing up our bakery products, my brother and I walked almost five miles to sell our bakery. We would also sell tea. Mainly, our customers were people walking the long distance from the mountains and remote areas and the villagers who were passersby and the porters. We had a good business selling bakery products, we used to make a good profit.

The porters and the passersby used to buy our products and were happy because they were able to satisfy their hunger after walking long distances. Our customers were happy and thankful to us even though they were intrigued that small children were handling this business.

On our first business journey from the border town of Dath Gari, India, we were able to sell all of our bakery products to the customers. We returned our sister's investment the first month and with the profit, we were able to continue our business. We also handled maintaining the books at the end of the day.

Riding a bicycle was my hobby from early childhood. I used to think of when I would grow up and have money and then I would buy a bicycle of my own. With the profits we made from the small bakery business, I managed to save up and buy a bicycle! My other sibling also learned to ride on the same bicycle. Sometimes, I would fall on the road after several riding attempts. Finally, I was successful at learning to ride a bike. Riding my bicycle for the first time was really exciting and enjoyable. I didn't even feel the pain from my scrapes and bruises; the joy was too great.

The success of our small bakery business really inspired me to dream of opening a bakery factory in my village.

As time passed by, one day our village head (Mandal) set up a meeting. In the meeting, all the villagers were invited and there was a mass gathering. My mother also attended the meeting. When it was over, my mom came home with tears of sadness on her face. I didn't understand then, but later I realized something might have happened at the meeting. Even so, I continued to pack bakery and heading to sell my products.

On the way, I was having different feelings, thinking about why she was crying. I had never seen a single teardrop in her eyes before, though she had to bear many responsibilities and had endured much suffering. She was a strong mother, if we said bad things, she always advised us to do good things and be positive to others. She also encouraged us to respect our elders and care for the younger people. She even insisted that we take care of the poor and needy. She used to say that "if we make them happy, in turn, God will also be happy and will give us blessings; the ability to help the needy is one of the greatest gifts God gives us."

Stealing and looting began to happen in those days. The same day as the village meeting, there was a group of vandals who came to our stall. They ate almost all of the bakery from our stall, including my friend's bakery. They made us prepare tea for them again and again and, when we asked for money, they started threatening us and tried to beat us up. Luckily, we escaped from the scene with our lives. After that, we were afraid that they would return, and we closed our bakery business.

The next day, I asked my mom why she had been crying that day and she told us about what happened at the meeting in Mandal's house. He divulged that we had to leave our country within two months. I realized why my mother was crying. Mandal told her that she no longer had any rights to any of our land or businesses. He let her know that our property was being seized by the government and that her children would have no rights to go to school and her family members would not get a NOC (Non-Objection Certificate) for study or to travel in Bhutan. Mandal announced that our relatives who lived in Chuwabari (our uncle's family) had already left the country without the government's consent. He told her that it was not a good idea for her family to stay in the village, she needed to leave as soon as possible.

Mandal told us there was a provision by which we could receive money from Bhutan's government. If we would leave the country voluntarily by the date given; if we would register at the Sharbhang Dzong (office); if we would fill out the voluntary migration form, then, after filling the form they would give us travel fare to leave Bhutan. Sacrificing property, accepting nominal amounts for our land; they also insisted that if the situation improved within six months then we could return to our country.

At that time, our house was less than a year old. It was built with great effort by my mom and my elder brothers and sisters. When we were forced to leave, we had to abandon our new house, our properties, our land, and our crops, and our domestic animals. Neighbors and relatives came to say goodbye. It was one of the most difficult situations I have ever faced; to leave my lovely country Bhutan and my beautiful village Toribari where I was born. Most of my family members cried as they packed to leave the country and our neighbors and relatives joined in.

It was the 21st of July 1992 when we joined two other families from the village to reserve a truck for our departure. We loaded it with our family and all of our worldly possessions. As we waved goodbye to our village, the truck began its journey to Jhapa, Nepal. That moment was very painful and incredibly difficult for my mother and elder siblings, but for me and my younger siblings, it was a time of innocence and ignorance about the storm that was brewing. We were having fun and playing happily inside the truck while traveling. On the way, we stayed one night in India, and the next day we arrived at Kakarvitta, the border between Nepal and India. We registered there and were given permission to enter one of the refugee camps. The staff from the registration office directed us to go to Goldhap Refugee Camp in the eastern part of Nepal.

4

FROM ONE CAMP TO ANOTHER

When we landed at Goldhap Refugee Camp, I saw another group of people from the other side of the village departing from another truck. One of the guys from that truck was arrested and taken away. I was shocked and anxious to see that happen. Rumor had it that he was a spy. There were thousands of people and as many huts made of bamboo poles and tarpaulin plastic roofs in the refugee camp. It was hot and sunny the day we entered the refugee camp. I was very thirsty and drank a sip of water from a tube well. The smell of the water was very horrible, and it tasted like decayed rotten iron. These were my first impressions of the refugee camp. I realized that we had come to hell.

My elder brothers and sisters, and two other families who came with us started unloading the trucks and started building our hut in a small space between two other huts. This was the only space that was not already occupied.

That night, my mom and the smaller children stayed in one of our uncle's huts who had already come and been settled in for a while. From the next day forward, we slept in our own hut. We were the last group of people to arrive at Goldhap Refugee Camp. Going forward, people arriving from Bhutan were taken to the refugee camps in Beldangi.

Two of our friends accompanied us on our journey to the Goldhap Refugee Camp and stayed with us for about a week. While they were there, we were eager to watch a movie to refresh our bittersweet memories of Bhutan and I, along with my friends and my brother, went to watch a Nepali movie entitled Didi at Birtamode in Jhapa, Nepal.

After a couple of days, my family members returned to watch the same movie while my two friends returned to Bhutan. We never saw each other again and had no way to communicate with each other. When we first arrived in the refugee camp, we set up a temporary hut but there was no proper infrastructure such as toilets, hospitals, water, and other basic facilities.

Most of the people who suffered from the epidemic diseases such as dysentery passed away. The very young and the elder person were particularly hard hit. They lost their lives due to the terrible conditions caused by cramped living conditions and the lack of available medical treatment.

Due to the influx of refugee arrivals in the eastern part of Nepal, the UN (United Nations) took the initiative to support the refugees in the camps. The World Food Program, UNHCR (The United Nations High Commissioner for Refugee), SCF (Save the Children Fund), AMDA-Nepal, LWF (Lutheran World Federation), Caritas Nepal, and other partners supported the refugees by providing basic infrastructures and necessities. We were provided rice by the World Food Program through LWF. UNHCR administered the camps and provided kerosene and vegetables, and

LWF provided bamboo for huts and roofs. Some basic health facilities were provided by AMDA-Nepal while, lastly, CARITAS Nepal started schools in the camps.

There were huge gatherings of people everywhere. The huts were very cozy and congested. There were constant robberies as well as people fighting each other. Domestic violence was common, as well as sexual violence and human trafficking. The situation was alarming and seemed hopeless.

As time passed, we didn't live, we just existed in the refugee camp. Educated individuals came together jointly to start the school program in the refugee camp in the open area. I remember waiting anxiously for school to start. Eventually, I joined the school in Goldhap camp within a few months of our stay there. The school was set up according to the class system. Once it started, a ray of hope began to emerge.

I never gave up hope that I would be able to attend classes regularly again to learn. My mother was the one who was the happiest knowing that there was a future for us. During this period, we didn't get textbooks to read but I had a friend who got a book from his previous refugee camp (Maidhar). I was enrolled in the third grade.

During our transitional phase at the Goldhap Refugee Camp, my elder brother Dhan opened a small grocery business at the bank of a small river. After school, I used to help my brother, while he was out to get more items for the shop. Eventually, the refugees who did not have accommodations and were living in temporary huts had to move to one of the camps in Beldangi. We stayed at the Goldhap Camp for six months and then we moved to Beldangi, where life was much better than at the previous one.

We got a plot of land and my elder siblings and my mother constructed another new hut, similar to the previous one at Goldhap. It was made of bamboo and the roof was constructed of plastic.

Life in the refugee camp was full of misery. We had to endure the rainy season which was unimaginable. In the beginning, it was really hard to figure out our own hut too just because all the huts were identical. During the windy and rainy season, we needed to hold down the plastic roof but sometimes, a gust of wind would blow it away and we had to stay without a roof until we got new plastic. When it was raining, most of the water permeated the inside of the hut, sometimes overflowing the water from the drain. One bright spot was the water tap that was built giving us tasty water in this camp compared to the previous camp.

Because of the densely populated refugee camp, people struggled to get water in the morning and evening. Water taps were distributed per the sector population. In one sector there were 300 to 400 people.

Within two to three months in Beldangi Camp, I remembered, my second sister Hari had married Ganesh Pradhan (my brother-in-law) from Pathri camp. All the children from our family, including my elder brother, joined the school at Marigold Academy in Beldangi II Extension (camp). Here, I was admitted to the fourth grade. We started studying on the ground under the trees but later CARITAS Nepal and the UNHCR built a school.

After the school was built, we started our education sitting on the floor under the thatch roof surrounded by bamboo walls. We carried sacks to sit on and smeared the floor with mud and cow dung once a week to make a clean floor and to keep the dust from blowing.

We had to do semi-annual and annual exams in school. Though we didn't have a good infrastructure nor concrete buildings, we had hardworking teachers who gave us the best education available during those critical days. Most of our teachers received their education from Bhutan and some from other countries. I made good friends but only had a limited number of best friends who were constantly in touch and close to my family. Some of my friends became very close and we enjoyed watching movies together in a nearby city called Damak.

We used to scrape up small amounts of money to watch movies sometimes. We would walk almost seven kilometers (more than four miles) in anticipation but when we arrived, we never had such a thing called snacks and drinks to enjoy while watching the movies, it would have been beyond a luxury.

Due to our poor health and lack of hygiene people would get sick easily in the camps. Malnutrition was the main cause of our sickness, but air pollution used to be another big health hazard.

My mother was working very hard for the welfare of her children and equally for other people. She would weave blankets and knit sweaters to earn a living and to buy basic needs for our home and for guests who would visit us in the refugee camp. My mother treated all her guests as if they were God, showing them respect and good manners.

There was a culture of going on picnics once a year either through our school or by our neighbors and relatives. That would be the most fun thing we would do! At a riverbank or in a small jungle, we used to have music, dancing, cooking under the open sky, and eating from banana leaves.

My first labor job was at a construction zone during my winter break. Most of my friends couldn't do the job but I stayed to earn some money and help my mom support our home. It was the most difficult time I faced, hiding all of my pain and tiredness in front of others. I had to come to rejoin school after two months of seasonal work, where I had earned 3000 rupees (about US $25), the first and greatest earnings of my life. I gave all the money to my mother, but she insisted that I keep some for my personal expenses.

In ninth grade, we had to go to another high school named Tri-Ratna where students from different camps would congregate. I had the opportunity to meet with many friends from different camps and did not notice how fast two years passed. In tenth grade we faced our iron gate, it is the hardest year for the students to pass, almost all the students had exam phobia after hearing how tough the test was, and each and every student were serious minded and focused on their studies.

I joined Siddhartha Higher Secondary School for my High school and studied Commerce with my refugee friends. It was very tough for us to choose between subjects such as Science, Commerce, and the Arts. My sister Damanta who was working for UN-WFP (World Food Program) encouraged me to study commerce as our parents had business experience and, more importantly, in order to carry on their legacy. This interested me though, being a refugee, we didn't really have any choice.

Whatever subject we studied, we had to become a teacher either at a private or at the refugee camp school. Our only option as a refugee was to complete our training and start teaching. I shared a rented room with my friends to complete high school which was economically difficult.

Soon after I finished high school, I served a year teaching in the same school that I graduated middle school from in the camp. I started earning 731 rupees ($6.26) as a monthly incentive which was used for my family and me. In the meantime, I earned my bachelor's degree in Commerce at Mahendra Morang Campus in Biratnagar, Nepal. After teaching for one year, I went to Birtanagar to further my education; staying with my friend who was a science student.

In college, I shared a room with friends, but it was a different experience. It was a little further from the camp so I couldn't come home often. I started doing a little part-time job as a tutor to local children which was immensely helpful in meeting my personal expenses.

Throughout my school years, the title "Refugee" was a bitter pill we had to swallow because people felt that refugees didn't have anything and had no rights to do anything. They were judged and treated differently. Amidst this reality, I never gave up on my dreams and hoped that one day that word would be removed from me.

Soon after completing my bachelor's degree, I started teaching at a private school away from home in the bigger cities in Dharan and Kathmandu respectively where I began my master's degree (Postgraduate) at Shanker Dev Campus.

5
SECOND ZONE PEOPLE

During the summer and winter breaks, we used to go to work all day near the local villages to pull weeds and grass from the fields. The locals didn't treat us well because of our status. We knew we would not be treated well even though we were cheap labor. We were never paid what they're promised us. At the end of the day, we were paid a few rupees less due to the circumstances. That's when I realized that the value of human beings depends upon the status. We have been abided by different circumstances which lead to carry out despite discrimination.

Life in the camp was so miserable, there were a significant number of the refugee population that were malnourished and sick due to an inadequate supply of nutritious food. Many lives were lost due to a lack of good sanitation, safe drinking water, and guards against disease outbreaks. Open fields were used as toilets for hundreds of people. The weather and climate didn't suit us, which was another reason for multiple health issues. The food provided in the camp was insufficient for those families who had young growing children.

UNHCR administered goods under camp management, providing us with the basic needs: vegetables, kerosene oil to cook and light in the night. In addition, we used to collect dried leaves and wood chips in the nearby jungle as the kerosene provided was always insufficient. We were told the oil should last us two weeks, but it was not enough to last us one. It was a risky job gathering the wood chips and dried leaves, many of us were either caught and beaten by the local authorities or the wood we collected was taken from us.

I spent most of my childhood and adolescence in the refugee camp. Those 16 years of camp life were unforgettable but that was where I learned many valuable lessons that I will never forget. If I hadn't gone through all that suffering and hardship, I wouldn't be here who I am today, although I will wish no one to experience this. Humanity matters the most, that's the sole lesson I learned there. No matter how rich or poor you are, respecting each other is the utmost one human being can do for another. I have seen how pathetically rich and educated people treat the poor and needy and am saddened by it.

Poor people had to work on the rich people's farms with the agreement of distributing a percentage of their crops. But in case, if they didn't produce a good harvest due to natural calamities and were unable to reach the targeted goal. The investment of labor and time would be worthless. In the next session, the poor farmer had to fulfill the required percentage as well as what was remaining from the previous one. This was the bitter truth I had seen firsthand.

This is why debt continues to pile up on poor people, and if the parents are unable to pay it off then it goes to the children. This is how the poor remain poor from generation to generation. The poor people never saw happiness and never thought of a happy life, they were emotionally paralyzed. No one knowingly wants to be a second zone person, but it happens due to their level of understanding and the education level among their people.

Rich and poor both have life and live in this universe for a certain period of time. No one is immortal. Everyone has to leave this earth someday; the only difference is the timing. Rich people have to treat poor people well and respect their work. God has created all human beings equally and they must be treated equally.

Gender discrimination was also practiced in society. Due to male dominated society, people were unable to see proper economic development. There was no concept of equality and equity in the earlier days. People thought that women were biologically vulnerable, and they should be prohibited to go out and work. Education for females was a distant dream. It was believed that women had to work inside the home to cook and bear children. For a secure family, both husband and wife are equally important to build a life together. They are like two sides of the same coin. If good education was provided to women, they could do as much as men. The only difference is biological from birth. For example, in most countries, women are in high-level positions running the administration of NGOs (Non-governmental organizations), INGOs (International non-governmental organizations), and even the government offices. I have also observed that some developing countries' have caste or class systems, systematic racism, and many other problems but at the end of the day, it's one human being treating another human being in the wrong way. But change is possible.

6

DEPARTURE TO AMERICA

After several rounds of bilateral talks between the Bhutanese and Nepalese Governments, there was no hope to go back to our homeland. Finally, the IOM (International Organization for Migration) along with the UNHCR decided to resettle the Bhutanese refugees to the United States, Canada, Australia, Netherlands, and a few other European countries. We were ecstatic to start the process of resettlement. It took almost a full year to complete the process which included several interviews, health screening, and documentation. This fulfilled all the overseas processes and finally, we were approved to come to the United States of America.

In our family, my youngest sister Nithya, myself, and my elder brother Dhan's family, his wife Sujata and daughter Drishya, were the first group to fly to America. We completed the screening process and cultural orientation. We were very happy to leave the camp and start our new life in America but there were many uncertainties in the new world. We were given a very short notice of three days to fly to Kathmandu. That's where the tension began, our relatives came with many different opinions. Despite all of this, we were so excited to travel to the US. My mother performed every ritual for our safety and good wishes in America before we left. Those three days and nights were the most memorable of my life.

On the departure day, neighbors, relatives, friends, near and dear ones were in line to bid us goodbye; I couldn't hold my tears back. One life was ending but a new life was beginning. I managed to console myself to keep myself strong in the new country.

The charter plane was full, there were no more seats, and my family members were told to go onto a commercial flight. This was my first time flying on a plane and it was really exciting, but at the same time stressful. It was a small domestic plane full of people, traveling over mountainous areas, having many spectacular views of clouds and mountains. Eventually, after three hours, we arrived at Kathmandu Tribhuvan International Airport. We were transported to a transitional place in Kathmandu for three days. Staff from IOM checked our vitals and shared pre-departure information as well as reiterating the cultural orientation information again at the transit point.

Heather, a Canadian citizen, young, energetic, and tall girl who studied in Brussels and did an internship as an escort from IOM, guided and mentored us during our journey from Kathmandu to Brussels, Belgium. She explained to us all the basic accommodations and adjustments that are needed on the plane. I was asked by our escort to interpret in the Nepali language to refugee families on the plane. It was quite an interesting journey as she was explaining to us all sorts of things on the plane. Her guidance made us easy transiting throughout our journey.

All the passengers boarded the plane including my family members and other refugees. The Airline Stewardess demonstrated how to fasten the seat belt and also announced where the emergency exits were. They also announced that the plane was ready to fly towards Delhi, India. We flew from Kathmandu to Delhi which was about a two hours flight. The layover there was difficult because it was so long. We spent twelve hours in Delhi, trying to sleep, to eat, but nothing worked. My mind was full of questions and uncertainties but also enthusiasm. Dinner was provided at the airport but most of the group didn't eat. Some of the elderly in our group were from a Brahamin family and were prohibited by their religion to eat food cooked by other people. They were whispering amongst themselves that they didn't eat food cooked by people from other cultures. I saw them eating only some dry food. Sometimes, religion and beliefs can fail people, that's why it's wise to follow the applicable rules only.

Superstition and the caste system are still big issues in our culture though they are slowly fading away. The time has come to make a change in our society by bridging the gap of superstitious beliefs. Education is the only way for change to happen and our people need proper education that will enlighten our society and be a catalyst for future change.

Early the next morning, after waiting twelve hours at Delhi International Airport, the airline staff announced that it was time to check-in and make sure that everybody had their boarding pass in hand for the next flight. It was a long journey from Delhi to Brussels. We were provided a good meal while traveling. Our escort, Heather, continuously checked in with us during the flight to make sure everything was ok. We sat at the back of the economic compartment closer to the bathroom. I was surprised to see lots of people with different ethnicities talking in their own language. When we started hearing the alarming sound of the plane during the time of takeoff, I felt a kind of nervousness. I told the people in our group to remain in their own seats notifying the time to take off.

Finally, we landed in Brussels. Heather's job was complete. She said in Newark, New Jersey someone else would guide us. It was difficult for us to say goodbye to our escort because she had guided us a very long way and I appreciated all the help she had given us. As a token of love and respect, my sister Nithya and I gave her a handkerchief. We were sad but I felt that life had to go on and there was a living to be made.

Without an escort, we were helpless on the plane to Newark which was almost an eight hours flight. Things went pretty simply inside the plane; we ate whatever was provided and we followed the instructions given by Heather. In Newark, we had to show all of our documentation to the immigration and customs officers.

Our final destination was Cleveland, Ohio but our flight had already left, and we had to now go via Washington DC. We came across different perceptions at the transit. We felt that we are in a completely new world. We saw people busy in their own way with laptops, cellphones, others are walking hurriedly to reach their destinations I assumed. This turned my imagination to the feeling I had in the refugee camp before traveling.

With an unknown destination, with a scared feeling, I kept marching carrying IOM bags and handbags to catch the plane to Cleveland after inquiring at the ticket counter. When we finally arrived at Cleveland Hopkins International airport, a case manager from Catholic Charities and two Nepali guys, said "Welcome to Cleveland!" which was a great moment. We went to the baggage claim center and picked up our belongings; it was 11 pm.

It was a cold November day in 2008 when we arrived in Cleveland. The caseworker arranged for someone to cook Nepali food for us at one of the Nepali families, who had arrived in Cleveland before us. In the Bhujel family's apartment, we ate and had a good time introducing ourselves and getting acquainted with America. At that very moment, three Nepali men came to meet us, among them was one of my college friends. I was so happy! It gave me confidence and allowed me to start asking questions about this new place that was now my home.

I thought we would be staying with them overnight but, unfortunately, it didn't happen. We were taken to our apartment by the caseworker who taught us how to turn on the lights, how to operate the stove, showed us how to use the bathroom and the kitchen and where the bedroom was. Then he left us saying we will meet tomorrow morning.

My sister and I didn't sleep all night, we explored every corner of the apartment. Some clothes were hanging in the closet and some food in the fridge. There were bathroom necessities in the bathroom too. I started experimenting with how to use these items. Our beds were already made up, with a nice quilt, pillows, and bedsheets which we never had before. There were so many emotions running through our minds that we only had a few hours of sleep that night.

The next morning, the caseworker taught us how to use a microwave. Our experience with the microwave didn't go well. We tried to boil eggs for breakfast and put 2 eggs inside which ended up exploding everywhere. In the end, we ate only bread that morning. It was a story that we told to each newcomer and also a tale to tell and laugh about among friends and family. In the beginning, there were many challenges to face for newcomers in this new place. But it didn't take long for us to begin to understand the American culture and to adapt to our new country.

7

CLEVELAND MY NEW VILLAGE

On the third day after I arrived in Cleveland, our case manager took us to the Social Security office and Welfare office to apply for food stamps and a social security number. In our leisure time, we would shop at Giant Eagle, Marc's, and Family Dollar, along with our Nepali friends. Collectively, we were learning how to shop and finding different items within the stores.

Being a person who came from a place where there was hardly a general store, where there used to be cash only open street shopping, it was really challenging for us at the beginning. Slowly but surely, we learned how to shop, deposit money in the bank, use bank cards wisely and so many other new skills. Our knowledge level skyrocketed in those early days.

Our first Thanksgiving in America was a treat. The Indian community organized a Thanksgiving Dinner for the Bhutanese-Nepali Refugee families as a welcome dinner. We were really happy to see all kinds of food there but none of them tasted like food back in the camp. We were craving the spices from India and Nepal. Spices like, fresh chillies, turmeric powder, cumin seeds, fennel seeds, red chilli powder, and many more which we've been using since a very early age. The availability of spices was a hot topic to share with the family members back in the camp, which was also a plus point to the families who didn't want to come to the USA. Finding a new grocery store of our wants was most challenging. We wind up going to different places in search of stores where we find the commodities of our choice. Finally, we started locating some of the grocery stores, but it was most challenging to reach the same place again by taking the RTA bus.

One day, our mentor Mr. Zahid Siddiqi, an Indian-American. A former engineer but very active in the social service networks. The Siddiqi's have established and run a public charity "Salam Cleveland" took us to the Indian grocery store. We were beyond happy to find Nepali spices, chili, and other green leafy vegetables that we were missing. We bought more than we needed to make the food for the special dinner that day. When everything else around you are strange, finding the food that is familiar to you and reminds you of home is a great comfort.

The next day, he came and took us to find a job for the first time in Cleveland and taught us how to use public transportation. That day, my sister Nithya got lucky but not me.

During the temporary stay at the apartment, I was eagerly awaiting the arrival of my other family members and communicated with them through emails and phone calls, describing everyday life here in Cleveland. My elder brother was here with us in a different apartment. While we waited, my sister and I were busy learning about new places and carrying out our daily routines.

Meanwhile, I continued to look for an entry-level job at different companies. I spent days waiting for calls from them, but no calls came. I was desperate to find any kind of job. My intention was to earn some money and send it to Nepal for my family to do some last minute shopping for their travel to the US. While I waited, I started helping other families to interpret the paperwork that came from the government offices.

In the early days, the language was one of the biggest challenges for me, my accent and my English pronunciation didn't help with understanding. At one point, I thought my degree was useless but, in a few months, things were much better in both areas. It was my nervousness and frustration that didn't allow me to understand Americans. One day, I went to the office of Catholic Charities (MRS) looking for a job, I explained my background in education and my experience back home to my caseworker.

To my surprise, he asked me if I would be willing to interpret during medical appointments for other refugees. That was a million dollar question for me with a 100% YES answer. I started interpreting for the initial refugee orientation, Refugee Health Screening, and other regular hospital appointments. At times, things were a little difficult when translating medical terms, but I never stopped learning and implementing what I learned. After three months of doing interpretation, I was called to work in an Indian Restaurant, "Flavors of India" as a dishwasher part-time. I was over the moon to start my first formal job. My first paycheck totaling $100 was worth millions to me.

After two months at the restaurant, I was called to work at the IX Center. My position at the restaurant was replaced by my cousin's brother who was very new to America. It was winter time and I had to use public transportation, but the weather was the bigger problem! I had to wait for a long time at the bus stop. There were several times when my pants turned into solid ice while waiting at the bus stop. I managed to join a carpool with a friend who worked with us there at the IX center.

My supervisor was impressed by my work and asked me if I knew anyone who needed a job. I had a good number of friends and family looking for a job. I helped about twenty of my friends and community members to find jobs at the IX center. We would work 10 hours a day at $7.25 per hour. It was like heaven for us to earn money on our own. We never got a chance to earn money legally in Nepal as we were not allowed to work without citizenship. We made a good amount of money in six months as the work was seasonal. After the IX center, I started working as a janitor at Bethany Elementary School and Day Care.

Our mentors Luanne, Paul, Katie, and Amy from Building Hope in the City helped my family members to find a job. They also helped us to take ESL classes for learning English in our house and many other things for which we will be forever grateful.

Paul helped me to learn how to drive a car. Not only that, but he gifted a car to me also. Luanne, a videographer, made a documentary about us and a wedding video when I married my wife,

Saru. Katie, another mentor, helped us to develop our restaurant menu when we opened our first restaurant. We had decided to move forward with doing business in America as we had in Bhutan. We, as a family, collectively bought the restaurant I had been a dishwasher at for my first formal job in America, "Flavors of India". We bought this restaurant in our first eighteen months in America.

One day Stacy Dever from Catholic Charities called us and told us about a job opening at ASIA (Asian Services In Action, Inc). Myself and my sister Bishnu applied for the vacancy. This was a much better job than I had been able to get to this point and where I am still employed to this day.

On one fine sunny day in my early days, I went to Akron to meet our relatives, and there I saw many refugees in need of help. I asked my manager, Susan Wong, if we could work in Akron also. She willingly said "Yes" and extended our position to work in the Akron office too.

One of the managers from Language Quill, an organization we worked with at ASIA, invited us to participate in a Public Health Awareness training in Columbus. I was told to bring two participants from our refugee community. That was my first time driving for a long distance on a highway.

As we drove, the road was blocked due to construction, and had to use a detour which was via the back roads. While coming back home, I was caught by police on the way; this was another first, my first ticket from the police. Having two firsts happen on the same day was very funny. My mentor Paul taught me what to do if the police pulled me over, I did exactly what he said and stopped in the right lane. The reason I was pulled over was for speeding which I suppose I did out of nervousness.

8

SECRET LOVE STORY

I was a senior in high school when Saru joined it in the eleventh grade. We did not know each other well. I saw her once in the tenth grade when we were introduced by my friend's sister. I saw her that day at school and to my surprise, her rental room was in the same building as mine. Being a year older than her and being from the camp, I started helping her and her friend with the initial phase of renting and living away from their parents for the first time. We started going to school together, eating together, and going to the grocery store together. In a short period of time, we became very close friends.

One day, she took me to her house, and I had the opportunity to meet her parents. After meeting them, I dreamt about my life with her. She was just so perfect in so many ways and I knew she was the one for me. I also took her to meet my family. I was blown away by seeing how respectfully she talked to my family that day.

We knew that we liked each other but were waiting for a good opportunity to express our feelings. My roommates started asking me, "what are you waiting for?". I saw the same spark in her too. I was away from her for the whole day, I missed her so much and realized that was a perfect time to tell her. I saw the same feeling in her when I got back to the room; that's where our love story began. Eventually, Saru was scheduled to attend a seminar in Thailand and had to leave for three weeks.

During those three weeks when my attachment for her and my longing to see her hit me hard, I was pretty sure the same thing happened to her. Our closeness was very obvious after she came back. Again, the story took another turn, when she had to leave for India for higher secondary school and college on a scholarship that covered her education for five years.

We started meeting once a year or sometimes twice. I completed high school and joined my college in Nepal. She completed high school and joined the college in India. We were waiting for the perfect time to admit our relationship to our family. In our culture, it was disrespectful to admit a love affair as our society still preferred arranged marriages. Our means of communication were emails and a few phone calls in the course of a year or sudden visitations from me as my younger brother was in Kalimpong, India doing his high school also.

She was my first love and my first girlfriend. I never considered finding another girlfriend. I had faith in our relationship as we were both committed to making the effort to maintain it. We would talk about making our love story an example for others; we didn't stop our education; we didn't run away from our responsibilities and we didn't cross any lines either. We didn't want to bring heartache to our parents because of our love story but we also were attempting to stand on our own two feet. We had decided together to work towards our parents' happiness and their betterment. Slowly, every relative knew about our bond and both sides of the family formally accepted our relationship.

During the entire eight years of our relationship, we had some ups and downs, but we always tried our best to make it work and vowed to make it a lifetime commitment. We didn't marry in Nepal even though our parents were ready to accept who we were. We were the ones to put it on hold until we got to America. We didn't want to start a family in scarcity in the camp.

Saru and I were in America less than one year when we were finally married. We were the first Nepali couple to be married here in Cleveland in our traditional manner as well as the first to get married in court in accordance with American laws.

It was so different from what life had been in the refugee camp. Even though we weren't sure that we could marry according to our culture and traditions in America. This was the happiest day of my life, to marry the love of my life in our new country, our new home surrounded by our friends and family. This made our happiness complete and truly began our new life in America.

I felt like marrying Saru completed something inside of me. I was blessed to marry the girl of my dreams and in such a way that we were able to set a good example for the community and all. When I thought about how weddings were performed in the refugee camp, outside in the space between two huts I couldn't help but be thankful for our mentors who did the wedding video and for the hall where we held the reception.

Our wedding video, made by our mentor Luanne, was a testimony to so many in the camp who were unsure about coming to America, restrictions here on religion, culture, and traditions. We sent many pictures to friends and relatives in Nepal just to encourage them and let them know that they can practice any religion and follow any culture here.

Mom: The Cornerstone

My mother is my living god. I know of her many sacrifices for her children to make them worthy of this universe. Despite her deteriorating health and poor financial situation without a husband and father for her children, she never gave up hope that she could raise her children well. She tried her best to give us love and care, and our mother played a dual role. She has immense faith in worshipping and does so on a daily basis until now for the betterment of one and all.

I cannot imagine losing your husband at the tender age of 38 with eight children to feed. Your spouse and the breadwinner suddenly bidding goodbye from this beautiful earth; my mother had to shoulder all the responsibility on her own during that time. She used to tell us that she felt like the sky suppressed her and the god was impartial to her. She is a very strong willed woman, rejecting her first marriage arranged by her parents and marrying my father who was the love of her life.

Marriages, within the same caste, were very important at that time. It is the traditional belief from the ancestor that they encourage to marry within the same caste. Preference was given to those who get married to the same caste, but she broke that norm too. You don't get married within the same caste, you don't get attention and care as the one who does from both sides of the families.

One day, after our school was permanently closed in southern Bhutan, my class teacher and her husband came and asked my mother about taking me with them to continue my schooling, and in return, I would do kitchen chores. She strongly denied that proposal, instead, she told them, "I can take care of my children and their education." At that time, it was common in our village for parents to give their children away to continue their education.

In May 2009, I was married which meant I now had additional family members. My in-laws are my close family members. They are very close to my children too. I felt so lucky to have my father-in-law as my own father as he was a very caring and loving gentleman. In the same way, my mother-in-law is as caring as my own mother.

I am always proud to be the son and son-in-law of the best mothers on this earth. Mothers are the sources of power to lead a successful life. They have a heart like an ocean where they can fit everything and bear anything for their children.

Meanwhile, in Cleveland, my father-in-law passed away from cancer within his first year of leaving Nepal and coming to America. Sadly, we didn't get to spend enough time with him. Once again, I lost a father figure which broke my heart. He had a divine heart, a pure mind, and a strong work ethic. I can still feel his presence as a blessing in everything I do. There are things that we have to carry with us from our parents and I have so many good memories and examples of good deeds to follow from my father and my father-in-law. But life must go on and a living still had to be made.

We worked hard and struggled a lot to make our lives better than before. In the course of time, we became the parents of two beautiful boys, Shayne (10) and Seann (6). The addition of children made our lives a little busier and harder to balance but things are much better now as we have grown personally and as a family and the children are doing well academically.

9

BUSINESS EXPERIENCE

Business is the passion of our caste. Our Nepali culture is organized into a caste system per our profession. Most of our caste in Nepal were businessmen for generations. Like the Patel caste in India, and the Newar caste in Nepal.

I am a person with a business mind and a social heart. I want to keep myself busy creating business opportunities and giving back to the community unconditionally and with a pure heart for the betterment of people's lives. It is important to grow, learn and develop a culture of good lessons and a value of giving back to the community.

From childhood watching my parents, I grew up in a business environment and I learned business concepts in my college too, which influenced me to start a business.

In 2011, a time of recession in the US, our family planned to open a restaurant by pooling our savings. With limited knowledge about business in this new country, we talked to our mentors who were surprised that people so new to America had adequate knowledge to begin a business venture of this magnitude. With our great enthusiasm and courage, we decided to start the business. Our mentors guided us in the beginning on how to run the business and also introduced us to different people and resources on how to operate the business. My son was only one year old when the business opened, and I did not have enough time to play with him.

I was working 9 a.m. to 5:30 p.m. at Asian Services in Action helping refugee and immigrant families in Cleveland and Akron for benefits, employment, and housing assistance to meet their basic needs. Right after work, I used to go straight to the restaurant. I would start serving customers and washing dishes; whatever was needed. After the restaurant closed, I would manually prepare the sales report; during this time, I worked almost 18 hours a day.

With my busy schedule and the myriad of responsibilities for the newly arriving refugee families, it was quite challenging for me to give quality time to my kids. Doing business in my new country was not a joke; it was hard work. But we managed to run our restaurant in North Olmsted; eventually, due to the heavy workload and a lack of time, I couldn't continue my restaurant business and I turned it over to my extended family. As time passed, I started adjusting my daily life and began to make plans to open a grocery store.

Due to the growth in our community in Greater Cleveland, there was an increased demand for a local Nepali grocery store that would sell food and items from home. We, my siblings, and I started the South Asian Grocery under Pradhan Enterprises on the West Side of Cleveland in 2012. When I first came to Cleveland, it took almost a month to get the Nepali spices to acquire that flavor of Nepali taste.

We started delivering Nepali spices to our community right after the arrival of the new people in the Cleveland area. The store became a meeting hub for new people and a place to share their sorrow and happiness amongst each other which reduced their anxiety and stress. Meeting with other Nepali speaking people helped to reduce the impact of cultural shock experienced after arriving in a new country. In the beginning, for those who did not have a car, we provided transportation services too.

This is the country of abundance and the land of opportunity. We started serving the community with the goal of meeting their urgent needs. It helped to create employment opportunities and we contributed to the economy by paying taxes. A small business like ours struggles a lot to sustain itself and survive in this country. The investment of time and hard work are the crucial ingredients to success, along with following all the government compliance and regulations. It is difficult to compete on price with bigger stores like Giant Eagle, Marcs, Sam Clubs, and many others.

Teamwork plays an important role in achieving success. In order to be competitive, we had to drive seven to eight hours to New York every week to buy products for the store. In the beginning, I, along with my elder brother Dhan and younger brother Narayan, used to drive to New York. Early in the morning, we had to compete with others to get fresh vegetables as many other Nepali businessmen from other cities and states also went to New York for the same reason.

During the winter night, it was very difficult to drive in the snow through Pennsylvania. The road was covered with snow and it was difficult to figure out where the road was. I almost drove the van off the road and into a valley more than once. I narrowly escaped a major accident multiple times. When we brought the product to the store it would take us about eight or nine hours to drive it back from New York.

Sometimes, we would have to throw out some of the product due to unfavorable weather conditions. We felt like we were living examples of Darwin's Struggle for Existence theory and Spencer's Survival of the Fittest supposition. We continued to struggle and never gave up even as we loaded and unloaded our grocery items in the middle of the night. It had the added benefit of providing us with exercise and keeping our bodies physically fit.

People felt that we were "lucky" and "successful", but they did not see the blood, sweat, and tears we invested along with the long nights of work required to make the store successful.

Everyone can make a difference in their life if they work hard and with passion. We had to listen to complaints and make corrections in order to improve our customer services and better serve our community. The best part is that we did not have to go to the gym; loading and unloading the trucks, mopping the store, and stocking the shelves are the best exercise we could have to remain healthy.

In due time, we started Himalayan Restaurant at the beginning of 2020. Just after opening the restaurant, the COVID-19 pandemic began. Despite adversity, we have kept running the restaurant according to the government order and regulations. There have been many challenges while coping with a pandemic. We continue to run the restaurant with reduced hours; serving our traditional Nepali and Indian food to meet the demand of the customers.

We have received immense support from the city, valued customers, Global Cleveland, Intra-National Welfare and Support Foundation of America Inc., along with coverage from ABC news during this difficult time. We will once again promote our Nepali food and culture once this situation improves. We would like to thank our valued customers and many individuals who have supported us during this difficult time. The whole world is suffering. Life has been drastically affected all over the world. As we know, there are many ups and downs in life; some feel like you are climbing the Himalayas, but we need to move our journey forward keeping our eyes fixed on our goals.

10

MY PASSION TO HELP OTHERS

From my childhood, I always had compassion for humanity. and an idea that it was very important to help each other to change the world. When I was in primary school, I got the opportunity to hear the story of Mother Teressa, her good works touched my heart. When someone says something, we might easily forget it but if we see the action and copy it, we can make a huge impact. Never be lazy to help the needy one, you will be rewarded for it in this life or the next.

I am one of the blessed people who have been able to serve the needy since I arrived in the United States. I feel like serving those in need is a way of serving God. If I make them smile, the whole world will smile, and it will bring me a better life. We cannot help all people but only those who seek our help. Without any conditions, we must serve the needy people verbally or physically to add value to their lives and teach them to live their life meaningfully.

In my life, I got help from individuals, mentors, and agencies as well as the United Nations to bring me to this place. Without their help and support, I cannot imagine what my life will have become. The world is a community, and we need to express solidarity. Helping people must be the rule, not the exception. Each of us must find a way to be a blessing to someone else.

Life is a service. Helping is not for creating dependents but a culture of work and independence. In the beginning, we have to help because people are in an emergency situation but after a time, we have to teach them how they can be self-sufficient. "Asian Services in Action, Inc." and "Refugee Services Collaborative of Greater Cleveland" (RSC) set a pioneer example. Under their leadership, during my twelve years as a social worker, I have been working tirelessly to build a culture of self-sufficiency and independence so that the younger generation can follow my example.

It is not appropriate to use other's suffering to build yourself up as a false image of a savior or rescuer, taking advantage of weak people or people in need. People need help due to a lack of knowledge or ignorance. Those who are taking advantage of needy people will have to bear the consequences of their actions in their long life. We need to be helpful to needy people without keeping any preference.

Love must be the motivation of giving; without love everything we do is valueless. Our heart has an ocean of love, we can give as much as we can respect every individual. When you serve others or if you give anything, give with a pure heart that helps to create a beautiful environment in society.

My job as a social worker has taught me a valuable lesson about individual's lives from diverse cultures. We are people with pure hearts. We all are born on this beautiful earth to make better earth but due to the bad environment and ill behavior of a few bad people, life is polluted for the innocent people who are made to suffer.

I was one of the lucky individuals to get hired at Asian Services in Action, one of the Social Service agencies in Northeast Ohio, and in collaboration with various agencies, I have had the opportunity to work with great leaders and serve diverse people groups.

In the beginning, I was working with school children at an after school program helping kids with their homework. During the daytime, I was working at a self-sufficiency department to assist people applying for benefits and also interpreted for clients as needed. People who came from developing countries needed lots of help to get settled in America. I had the first-hand experience of this and could bear witness to this fact, that is why I worked tirelessly to serve my beloved people and those who needed my help from diverse communities.

I also worked as a farmhand through a program run by ASIA at Susan Smith's organic farm with my teams. We used to grow mostly organic Asian vegetables and attended various seminars and training to learn how to grow vegetables in the United States when the weather is not suitable for many types of crops. While doing organic farming, we had to follow strict rules and regulations and needed to keep track of every single detail. We also needed to learn how to grow Asian crops during the limited growing season in Northeast Ohio.

It is important to teach every individual that we need to learn to eat healthily and organically (without pesticides) because what we eat makes a difference in our health. Our health is very important in our day-to-day life. Due to ignorance and a lack of healthy eating habits, we are slowly spoiling our life day by day. People who have poor health have to suffer a lot and also, they are liable to be discriminated against. Building a culture of eating healthy in a family is a good start for a long and happy life.

For some people, it is difficult to manage morning and evening meals, but some others are consuming bad things and becoming addicted to unhealthy habits which can spoil their healthy life. Everyone should know the importance of their life. The life we are living now is the best life in this universe and we must live it with profound enjoyment and engage in healthy activities. We cannot get back the previous moment that passes by.

Because of a growing need, I shifted my work to helping people with benefits, employment, and housing. It was very tough to integrate new people in the United States in the beginning. People were facing language barriers and needed help in various sectors. People were not used to getting letters in the mail and the time frame is very crucial in the beginning phase. I faced these challenges and improved my new life in my new country without knowing anything.

I tried to help people from my core heart so that they did not feel helpless and embarrassed. Newly settled people need lots of help in various areas and also, people from foreign countries have a different mentality. If they do not get the necessary help, they think differently and impact their ability to build a beautiful life negatively.

In the beginning phases of resettlement, due to various circumstances, our community was deemed to have one of the highest suicide rates per capita in the U.S. Due to a family conflict, one of my innocent clients in Summit County committed suicide and a month later, there was a case study presentation at our Refugee Services Collaborative (RSC) meeting showing the high suicide rate among the Bhutanese-Nepali community. I attended as I am one of the RSC meeting participants representing my agency. I listened but I could hardly control my heart.

I disrupted the presentation because of my crying. I thought I am from the same community, I cursed myself asking why we were not able to help these needy people.

We were fewer families and did not know that we were going to have such a large community. We did not expect it when suicide cases increased in the community. Later, I came to know that suicide happens due to several reasons such as family issues, culture shock, lack of necessary help, lack of knowledge of the new environment, unmet expectations, being emotionally disturbed, and so on.

With the help of the US government, various nonprofit agencies and community leaders applied for grants and created programs to help combat these issues. It is very important to educate people and raise their awareness with educational training to reduce substantially this issue if not eradicate it.

This small help creates a great impact in the community and adds great value to their life. I am always taking the initiative to help the needy people along with other community leaders. In the first decade of my work in social service, I cannot feel tired of helping the people who seek help from me. I can help them the best I can from my sphere. If I cannot, then I can refer them to other sectors where they can get help. Sometimes, in the middle of the night, they call us for help and my brothers-in-law and myself provide it the best we can. I work during the day in the office helping people and, in the evening and weekend, working in the grocery store, helping my brother. While I am there, people come with their mail and ask for help. I manage my time and help them, same as my brother-in-law. He contributes even more than me to meet the needs of the people.

Do not be lazy to help the needy people, always remain active and contribute what you know, a small help is worth millions to the new people. Most of the newly arriving people are shy in nature and they do not express their feelings and sorrow. If they tell or express it, they will need to address their situation as soon as possible.

It is important to help people and teach them to learn and help others and make a culture of creating good habits. While working with a social work agency we need to follow their guidelines, but to get help for the needy people, we need to go the extra mile and contribute extra time to serve the people with satisfaction.

People come to this country with high hopes and a big dream, but everything is totally different here from developing countries. In the early days, everyone was lost in the middle of nowhere due to culture shock and other circumstances. During this time, people need the right help, so later they can contribute to the development of the nation as a productive citizen.

One of my responsibilities is to find employment for the clients. In the beginning, jobs were scarce, and it was difficult to get a job because most of the people had limited English even though they spoke other languages. When applying for a job, they did not get called for the interview and we would take the additional step to meet with Human Resources or the owner of the company and ask them to please help one of our clients with an interview and ultimately with a job. We would tell them that if they did not do a good job you can fire them. Some of the employers trusted us and gave them an opportunity.

Due to the hard work of the first people hired, they called us and asked for several other employees. Most of the refugees and immigrants are hard-working and eager people. Back in their country, they might be an engineer, doctor, or any other higher profession but when coming to the US everyone has to start over. They have the opportunity here to get a certification or to start work in manufacturing companies in entry-level jobs.

People have many responsibilities to fill, that is why most people end up with entry-level jobs. Only a few people among those who continue their education are lucky enough to get a white collar job. Many people are promoted to a higher position in the manufacturing companies and other hospitality industries but, currently, even people with limited English are getting good wages at companies such as Amazon. People do not need to be fluent in English to get a good job, they only need to have a good work ethic and understanding of the work rules and norms of the company.

I learned from my parents and others that life is a blessing, and service is the fuel that runs our lives with profound satisfaction. Education plays an important role to keep yourself updated and able to render better service. As Jim Rohn said, "Formal education makes you a living, and self-education makes your fortune". A college education is basic to one and all but, in life, self-education needs to be continued until the end of one's life to have a huge impact on oneself and the universe. Belief in service and education have a huge impact on our commitment and passion to make heaven on earth.

My last several years of life in Nepal were full of scarcity and misery but I never gave up; remaining busy, receiving education, surviving by doing hard labor, and teaching in private schools with limitations. Some days, there was not enough food to eat, no fresh fruits and nutritious foods.

Twelve years of my life have been spent as a social worker in the United States making a difference in the life of needy people and the community. With social work, it is difficult to run a family and be involved in and running the family business; it makes me crazy busy and I do not have enough time to contribute to my family. In the US, I do not have to worry about the nutrition and abundance of food but with the stress and lack of knowledge about healthy eating habits such as eating regular meals.

One day with the help of my younger brother, I got the chance to attend network market training and I got to learn inner peace of mind and how to take care of myself first so that I could help others. If we want to change others, we have to change ourselves first. I started looking at myself in the mirror and found that I was taking other's burdens and stress into my life but now I have learned to manage it even with the increasing demand for help from the needy people in the community. Our great community leader in Cleveland felt it was time to form a nonprofit to address the needs of the people.

After several talks and much discussion, the Bhutanese Community of Greater Cleveland (BCGC) Inc was formed in 2017. Gradually, leaders decided to address the needs of the people residing in different parts of Cleveland. This has helped abundantly to share the burden. They came up with different plans and objectives after brainstorming among the members of the organization. Still, they are providing different services to needy people despite the pandemic.

Gradually, the younger generation started achieving in the field of education. Some of them have even gotten admission into Harvard University, Yale University and are pursuing their education. In the coming generation, we might see a great achievement in every sector. This is after all the hard work and hardship. We have to make a great investment in education to bring changes for a better society tomorrow. In a short period of 10 to 13 years, resettled Bhutanese-Nepali individuals have made a profound impact and progress in each and every sector for the overall development of nations wherever they are settled around the globe.

11

LESSONS TO BE LEARNED FROM MY JOURNEY

Family is first and foremost and one has to keep harmony with each other with the utmost respect. We must spend our precious moments with our parents as much as possible. These moments are priceless, and their blessings are valuable to boost your confidence and growth. No one is guaranteed tomorrow, and life is very short so enjoy it.

Sometimes, due to situations and circumstances within a split second, we have to change our mode of living and always be prepared to adapt to the changing environment. No one knows what is going to happen next, we must know how to survive in any environment, survival is not easy. Healthy living and healthy eating habits are essential to long life. We have to take care of our good health which most of us have to figure out.

In the case of healthy and happy living, the things that matter are consistency in everything we do and eat. In the refugee camp, due to a lack of healthy food, people suffered from malnutrition and many health hazards. In short, the importance of proper eating and wellness plays a vital role in maintaining good health, and is important to provide this awareness to the ignorant community.

Every day, at least an hour of physical exercise and yoga adds great value to your psychological and emotional balance and maintains the inner peace of our mind. Physical health and psychological health are equally essential to live a happy and healthy life. Everyone has to learn to live a balanced life otherwise a lot of misunderstanding within a family occurs and divorce between a husband and wife and many more issues can be created which are not healthy for a family.

Time is very precious. Don't waste it without doing the tasks you value most. Enjoy life with family and friends and entertainment with full satisfaction, while working to focus on the greatest outcomes. As we know, time is irreversible; once it's gone it never comes back, so utilize it properly in a constructive way for the betterment of self and all. Let's not spend time on negative and illegal activities as every action has an equal and opposite reaction, so we will have to bear the consequences accordingly for the rest of our life. We are born to make a difference on this Earth in good ways, let's act accordingly.

The word education is the most attractive magnet in every human life. Everyone can achieve an education, without which people can become wild and spend a life full of suffering and obstacles. The earth is the home of all living beings and, to add value and explore its resources, only education dominates and creates a beautiful earth. If I didn't attend school during my time in the refugee camp, under the wet tree, and with a lack of school supplies and necessities, there's no way I would be where I am now, making an impact on people's lives.

I encourage everyone to acquire education which is a key point for success. Education has limitless potentialities. Right choices always end up in positive outcomes. We can start with a small kind of action and slowly and steadily it teaches us to move with full swings. When I came to the United States, I came with $100 that was given to me by my beloved brother-in-law Bhupati, who played my father's role.

After seeing the vulnerability of myself and my community in this new country, I started to volunteer. I decided to be a social worker, but I came to know that with only being a social worker, it is difficult to survive. So, I started taking action with other family members to run a business.

Since then, I have continued taking action to make a difference in people's lives and for the survival of myself and my family. People make excuses for not working and, as a result, they have to depend on welfare. This will never give them the full satisfaction of work in their life. The outcomes of hard work from your own hand are better than any offering from someone else.

As per Bill Gates, "if you were born poor, it is not your mistake, but if you die poor, it is your fault". My country, the United States of America is the Land of the Free and the Home of the Brave. The diverse cultures of the world make a common platform for us all to live in harmony. It is a country of rich cultures and it is important to value and respect the cultures of each other. It is important to learn about each other's good cultures and bring them into practice.

Some traditions in some cultures bring harm to society and have not been updated as time requires, and this situation has to be eliminated. One important feature of Nepali culture is helping people in grief and keeping older mothers and fathers in the house instead of sending them to the nursing home.

Parents are our god and show us the beautiful earth, so it is very important to develop the culture to give warm love in their old age, whereas parents must develop the same culture when children are young.

Traveling to various countries is an important part of people's lives. It does not only help to understand other cultures and people, but it also gives recreation and education. Each country has a unique attractiveness and lessons to learn. Whatever new places we explore, we have a lot more things to bring back to our place and incorporate them for the betterment and enhancement of the quality of life. It helps to broaden our limited knowledge and raise the bar of our vision. My domestic and international travels add great value and resources to my life and help me to live meaningfully.

In life, it is essential to take the risk to be a better version of yourself and to upgrade the quality of life. People must understand that every problem has a solution but only by being self-empowered, courageous, and valuing education can we solve it. Happiness and suffering are the byproducts of living, but the art of balancing each moment in life is a valuable lesson everyone must practice as cultural norms.

People must learn the pros and cons of egotism. If self-improvement is good for the welfare of all, in general, it also gives you positive rewards. Wherever you live in this universe either in developed countries or developing countries, there is limitless potential. Always "Dream Big" and start taking action from when you are small to when you grow with full dedication and commitment; neglecting all the obstacles, then success will knock on your door sooner or later.

Everyone is created to contribute their best and to add beautiful color to earth. Together we make a huge impact and create a loving environment for the betterment of all beings. I also experienced that we have a lot of challenges with healthcare, such as language barriers, poor health care from the country of origin, unaddressed chronic conditions, low health literacy levels and even being behind on immunizations, because of such challenges, it is important to bring awareness in the health sector too. Culturally, most of our people don't practice their routine check-up and at the end, when the individual is severe, then they have the habit of going to the hospital, which results in threatening their situation in life. It is important to maintain a healthy routine.

I heard that, if you can control it, control it, if you do not and become extreme then nature will control it. I don't know, is it nature or what? I have seen several ups and downs in my personal life, but this COVID-19 Pandemic is something that the world is experiencing this year. The Coronavirus has negatively impacted the whole world and made us speechless. It changes the dynamic of everything that human beings are used to. It has taken the life of many people. I want to respect and salute those who work tirelessly to keep us alive. I want to extend my hand in wishing peace and comfort to live in heaven to those who lost their life due to COVID-19. These are huge changes to human history.

The year 2020 is considered a psychologically and emotionally challenging year. We hope the year 2021 brings changes and refreshes us to grow with high hopes and new remarks for living a long and quality life. People have to live moment to moment in this current situation, but it is important to learn lessons from the past experience and not to make the same mistakes repeatedly to make a beautiful life.

In life, no matter what, we have to continue doing our day-to-day work even though no one is immortal. Every person you meet in life, treat and greet them with kindness. You never know if you will meet him or her again. If you want to give something to others, give with a pure heart. We know that every life comes and leaves the earth when its time comes. So, it is important to make the mark of a great legacy so that the coming generation and the children of future generations will value it and transfer it as a culture for the betterment of human life.

Made in the USA
Columbia, SC
15 June 2021